Nothing Beyond Love

SELIM PANDIT

Made with ❤ on the Notion Press Platform

www.notionpress.com

I am dedicating this book Nothing Beyond Love to all the lovers who love their beloved with their pure heart.

Contents

Preface

Depression and anxiety are becoming more prevalent in love in this present day.

Without this, we could fail to feel or comprehend love's appropriate path.

To spread comprehending of the sacredness of love is the goal.

Along with dealing with the post-breakup prospects and post-breakup melancholy.

Selim pandit

28.04.2023

Acknowledgments

Thanks to everyone who helps me and guide me to publish the book.

Sketch is Designed by Md Shaqueeb Ansari.

Also thanks to Abdul Matin and my all respected teachers who helps me a lot to publish this book.

Introduction

In this book Nothing Beyond Love describing about the love.

Why we feel sad in love?

How does sadness affect you after depression?

What aspects of love causes harm?

Describes about the possibilities after break up.

How do we comprehend the concept of falling in love?

regarding the psychology of love.

Can anything be possible in love?

Nothing Beyond Love

Selim Pandit

Chapter 1

The Depressive Stage

All of us have learned that love may be a hell or a heaven based on who experiences. It depends entirely on others instead of just on ourselves.

Now let's talk about the fact that falling in love is okay or does so the first time is like a monsoon of romanticism, but this depends on the individual or man's thinking. Speaking of those that appreciate what we see in our current environment or generation. Some people fall in love for any reason, some because they need a mate, and some because they are lonely. But the truth is that true love is something you cannot describe, imagine, or even feel that you are in love. It's not necessary to use a common statement like “I love you.” its nothing about formalities. It's a cruel myth that love cannot exist unless you confess your love for someone. However, the real meaning of this line plays a relatively minor part in a relationship. 'I love you' is not necessary word to express love.

You will only need one distance to grasp the meaning of love, feelings, and emotion. Your beloved (unknowingly) indicates the fact that you are unaware of your feelings for her. Firstly, it should be made clear that there are many different kinds of love in the cosmos.

Humans divide those categories based on their own mentality. In addition to couple's love, there are many other types of love, such as brotherhood love, sister love, father love, and humanity lover, but when we talk about couple's love, means romantic feelings or emotion for someone.

Do you know jealousness is also a part of love, but still the question is when you realize that you are in love with someone?

It's a suspicious or confusion about the mind set am i in love with her or not? Or it becomes habits of this person.

It can involve speaking at a specific time or moment, or meeting at a specific time or moment. But when you realize it, you start to feel quite sad, perhaps because your beloved can't see you or talk to you. Anger develops significantly when you're upset but you can't express it. Your heart begins to beat or you feel incredibly irritated, furious, or tense when this event is happening to you. Then you remember that you are in love with this person (you are going to addicted with this person means habit)

In this entire universe many of people don't know the knowledge about why we become sad? To explain about the cause of sadness in one word that is much more expectation from others. However, if our happiness depends on others, we will never be a happier person. If our expectations aren't fulfilled, we get unhappy or depressed. The same reason of depression of love comes from the word of expectation.

The truth is, we have no idea what is love? We might fall in love, but we have no idea what love really entails or what it is defined as. How can I be happy in love?

Love is a sensation that no one can adequately describe or express. Without the person whom you love, you can never experience such feelings from another person. Nobody can truly define love because it depends on our own mentality or personal experiences.

"Ishq tujhse itna huyi,
Ke waya na kar saku
Aur mohabbat tujhse itna ki,
Ke kabhi bhula na saku."

Every individual person has every individual definition of love according to their own experiences.

When you can pray for your beloved, it may be your beloved is with you or not but still you are praying for your beloved's happiness. That's define you are in divine love or eternal love.

Watching the happiness of your partner will make you happy. You will be the happiest person if you respect your beloved's wishes and can smile one your beloved's smile. Whether you are with me or not, the approach of heavenly love or eternal love will be when you may bless your beloved with affection.

All of us fall in love with someone in order to be happy (only for pure love), yet the majority of people or couples end up ruining their lives as a result of sadness, anxiety, overthinking, and love-related possessiveness. As usual, we begin our love stories with the purpose of happiness or being joyful, so why do we experience anxiety, depression, etc.?

Simply said, having too high of expectations and being overly possessive are ruining the next generation. In two words, we may also say that the young generation is dealing with the mental illness. Mainly when it comes to the end of the relationship (love) means breakup. It poses serious risks to our mental health. The majority of couples experience mental illnesses like depression, anxiety, overthinking, negative thinking, etc. However, the primary cause was as previously stated: greater possessiveness and greater expectations. This commitment is not included in the terms of love. When your partner fails to fulfil to your high expectations due to circumstance or any issue, you may become depressed or even overly possessive of her. This is a bad sign of love or for oneself.

especially in break up or end of relationship, you have to remember a relationship may end but love has no end. When a relationship ended, you thought that your partner would never leave you. However, when your expectations not fulfilled, your capacity for positive thinking greatly decreased and you started to experience melancholy and worry. When you concentrate more on your ex—why she left you, why they behaved that way—you feel more depression. Your brain's chemical reaction was impacted. You then begin to experience mental sickness. Additionally, you require medical care, psychological counselling, etc. If you are conscious of love or understand what it truly means, you will never experience depression. Previous pages covered possessiveness and expectations of others (especially the loved ones). You never experience depression if you are fully aware of the two words: expectancy and possessiveness. You won't experience depression if you have minimal expectations from your partner and avoid becoming possessive. Love yourself first, expect from yourself this two rules will make you happier person. Remember, you can't be a lover or to love someone if you can't love yourself first. You will never experience even the slightest bit of happiness, if your happiness and expectations are dependent on others. You will be the happiest person if those depend on you.

Emotional effect in love psychology is also included. You might need to be less emotional in love, in society, or anywhere else, but you shouldn't be an emotional fool. You will never be able to be the mentally strongest person if you are unable to control your emotions. You must have to control the emotion if you want to be mentally strong. This is the most significant aspect of happiness and to be mentally strong. Love possesses limitless power. A lots of direction, ways exist in love but you can’t identify what will happened with you in love or what situation will come that you need to face. For some people, love is like heaven, while for others, it is like hell. What is waiting for you is impossible to predict. Less expectation and not being overly possessive or emotional will help you be psychologically strong and a positive person, and will especially help you think positively.

If you follow those instructions and comprehend what true love is, you won't ever experience love depression.

Nothing is beyond love, and love makes everything possible.

Chapter 2

Intention of revenge

After a relationship ends, there are two different kinds of revenge after: break up one is positive and the other is destructive. Now we must understand why we intend to take revenge. Without possessiveness and excessive expectation, negative revenge is never encountered. Once upon a time, we were engaged to one another and could do anything for the beloved, but what situation led to your starting to take revenge now? In revenge of love means, betraying of your beloved according to your own mindset.

The end of a relationship is the source of all vengeful attitudes. Positive retaliation that could be beneficial to both you and your society. And the second one is negative revenge that is harmful for yourself and for the society. All forms of revenge occur after a relationship has ended. Before anything else, we need to clarify why we want revenge after a relationship ends.?

Once upon a time, we were willing to give our lives in order to happiness of our beloved, but as times, moments, and circumstances changed, also changed our attitudes. The current circumstance is that if "you leave me, I cannot tolerate your leaving, I'll hurt you and get revenge from you". That kind of revenge is harmful to both you and for society.

Second in the same situation, you sob quietly after your loved one leaves. The person who breaks down intention that, 'you leave me due to my financial situation or may be for any reason of unsuccessfulness, disability etc.'

"I will demonstrate my strength, power, and capability to you." Without thinking about to harm to the beloved, perceiving to success, motivate himself finding the reason of deficiency and starts to hard work to recover the deficiency. That is positive revenge, which is starting to work hard for success without considering harming anyone. It is beneficial to demonstrate one's power and capability as one aspires to higher levels of knowledge. Hard work and persistence in demonstrating for the one they leave leads him to get success. If the person's lover stays, it's possible that they won't be successful. with a single sentence to demonstrate to his beloved that he is capable of doing whatever to close the gaps reason of leaving the person. All acts of vengeance that serve simply to demonstrate to the victim's loved one that they are wrong and intend to realize his beloved that whom you left yes he also can achieve success he isn’t a ‘street romeo’. The person wants to make feel guilty about losing his beloved. Another reality is that it has an impact on society. For instance, a girl broke up with a boy she loved because he came from a lower middle class household. This is why the girl broke up with the boy; she might have done so under pressure from her family (those events are on trend for the present generation). He experiences a severe emotional collapse because of the actions of his beloved or because of his situation.

Everything related to sadness and the causes of depression was covered previously. You feel unhappy because there is so much expectation and possessiveness. This chapter's introduction looked at two potential outcomes of the element of retaliation after a breakup: positive revenge and negative revenge. In this situation, the individual can manage the emotion of saying goodbye to his beloved and comprehend the true meaning of love; as a result, he never engages in negative revenge mindset. The person keeps a little bit of expectation and shrink in little bit of possessiveness but the person feels the real meaning of love if he wants to take revenge he always goes through the way of positive revenge means without thinking to harm anyone, motivating himself and perceiving to get success. After breakup a possibility also happen that is unaffected means doesn't effect to him after leaving. After the breakup, these two occurrences were also well observed. In positive revenge, the victim is so silent that the success is screamed. If his beloved hadn't left him, he might not take any action or be unable to attain extraordinary success. It shows that achievement comes through losing his loves, and society gains a brilliant, successful person. Therefore, despite the fact that he failed at love, he was a successful citizen due to this. A typical person can attain extraordinary success and demonstrate that yes i can, for the cause of leaves of one person. This is achievable for three reasons: one, emotional restraint; second, making the right decision in this situation; and three, persistence.

However, the second possibility is also possible in that same situation. The second possibility basically states that a someone may become overly possessive with someone whom he loves and mainly he goes through the negative revenge ways. In reality, being too possessive makes the other person irritated. You believe that the person is ignoring you, but the real culprit is actually you, but you can't realize due to the reason of possessiveness. It's possible that your possessiveness is the only reason the other person is ignoring or neglecting you.

Finally, the person whom you love is going to leave you or start dating someone else, this could be due to familial pressure, personal preferences, or any other factors.

When you hear about the news of engaging of your beloved or you see your beloved's engagement with other, hormonal changes are noticed in your brain. When you first became possessive, hormonal and chemical changes began to occur, but you were unable to feel it. However, when you saw or heard about your loved one becoming engaged, you lost control on yourself and noticed major hormonal and chemical changes on your brain. In the beginning of a relationship, no one becomes overly possessive, but with time, when some of people become blindly involved in the relationship and gets possessive. When your beloved confirmed their engagement, your excessive possessiveness completely destroyed your capacity for pleasant thought.

First, get hopelessly and deeply involved in a relationship; this leads to possessiveness; as a result of being overly possessive, come great expectations, which indicates depend entirely on your partner. Sadness results from having high expectations, which leads anxiety, depression, and mental disorders can impact you. One situation is connected with other situation.

Because of this, your capacity for happy thought is completely broken, and you start to feel angry. Due to the reason of destruction of positive thinking capability and hyper mentality is started to convincing the all of his situation is totally responsible his beloved. He can't endure it when he sees his loved one communicating to someone else. The happiness of his beloved without him can’t endurable. He keeps trying to hurt his loved one. These attitudes and intentions are primarily the result of two factors: first, a lack of actual education; second, incorrect knowledge of love; and third, being overly emotional.

If we are able to experience or comprehend true love, neither of these possibilities will ever occur, nor will anyone be harmed or negatively affected.

“If you aren’t happy with seeing your beloved’s happiness then definitely you never loved the person or you can’t say yourself that you are a lover.”

Nothing beyond love because anything is possible in love.

"Tumhe bewafa kaise kahu,
Mera dil bhi koi kam nahin jata.
Jo dhadakta toh hai mere liya,
Lekin tadapta hai kisi aur ke liye.
Aur kya hi likhu ankhon ke baareme,
Jo dikhta toh hai mere liya
Aur rota hai kisi aur ke liye."

Chapter 3

Founder of Charitable trust

It feels like an awkward chapter to speculate on how this chapter would relate to love. You'll be shocked when you realise that love also offers those possibilities.

Basically, this behaviour, occurrence, or circumstance is associated to a rich man or someone from a highclass family who has achieved extraordinary success.

In two factor those possibilities can happen, one is demise of beloved and second one is ‘loosing your beloved’ due to any reason may be loose the beloved because of God wishes.

Even when destiny prevents the actual souls from coming together, couples still make every effort to get married. Nobody is aware of God's plan. After many efforts to join, they finally fail. No one holds the other responsible for their failure to understand or feel their destiny. They are able to unite on a soul level, but not on a social one. As a result, their psychological behaviour alters. they are constantly trying to make their loved ones happy. They put all of their effort towards making happy whom he loves, putting himself last.

In particular, this event signifies the founding of a charitable trust. However, I want to make it clear that not all of the founders of the trust are doing it out of love; rather, they are genuinely kind individuals who care deeply about society and want to see it develop. As a result, they established the Charitable Trust. But if the person is financially, emotionally, and heartily eligible, this possibility can also occur. This specifically occurred for the demise of a loved. When person is completely broken, there is nothing or anyone can do to help them heal, yet their love is so pure that no one can omit. After some moment he starts to compromise or understand that now the beloved is no more but love for his beloved is still in his heart. After the beloved's death, he always wished to bring the beloved happiness. After the demise of his beloved, the person's desire is still to see the beloved happy. Every religion claims there are two ways after death. This concept is the sacredness of love; the one who loves her constantly wants to see their beloved happy, even after she have passed away. Therefore, if he is financially able, begin making donations in memory of his beloved because of the happiness of the beloved after the demise of the beloved.

You may occasionally observe that he begins to manage an orphanage because the lover is happy. believe that God will be impressed, and his beloved will be in heaven. This is the holiness of love, and the individual grows incredibly giving and kind-hearted as a result. His contribution to society is supported by the entire community. Due to the holiness of love, society will gain since many homeless children and children without parents will have a home and an education. God may not permit the actual souls to be united, but in place of love, many homeless children receive a home and food. Society gains many advantages just for the affection and goodwill of the loved. The person truly begins to serve the community, give back to the community, and pray to God for his beloved. God might accept his work's, contribution to society.

In the path of love, anything is possible. For the love someone may achieve heaven after demise. Everything is possible when you're in love.

"Tujhse mohabbat kitna hai,

Yeh toh nahin jante.

Tu aab meri naaahi hai,

Magar yeh dil nahin mante.

Kaise samjhau dil ko jeena hai tere bina,

Kyon ki - mumkin nahin tera aur mera milna.

Sayed khuda ki sazish thi ye

-Tujhe nahin paana

Mauka milga toh khuda se bhi puch lunga,

Kya zarori tha

Tujhe meri kismat mai nahin likhna."

Chapter 4

Suicide attempt

Depression is the most typical tendency or issue in relationships or after a breakup. After some time, some of them who had just experienced heartache or a breakup committed suicide because of the failure of love, which is the grimmest act or worst example of a narrow-minded mindset. This also occurs because lack of true education, feel lonely, and lack confidence if we comprehend what love is, which prevents us from making this decision. Any mental or psychological disorder must have affected the person who has suicidal thoughts. In the chapter before, we discussed two factors that contribute to depression: one is possessiveness, and the other is psychological dependence on a loved one. Those who are depressed appear to have hallucination that they cannot survive without their loved ones as their depression increases (primarily due to increased depression caused by overthinking about the breakup, which increases day by day if the person can't recover from the circumstance). This is the most cruel approach in love. He becomes depressed because of false knowledge about love that is misleading. First, we must realize that when we fall in love, we become attached to the person in order to be happy with them.

In the beginning, we are all extremely pleased, but after a while in a relationship (not all relationships are included), our happiness and sense of fulfilment will depend on the other person, i.e. our beloved. Assume everything will go as planned, using the example of the boy. Now he wants that she will do what he wants but remember its not possible for anyone, someone will do everything what you want this is not possible. If this case is going to happen with you then you are in wrong way, for this reasons day by day you will get affected by over possessive. Being overly possessive might be very destructive to you. And you begin to experience various mental disorders, primarily depression, anxiety, and occasionally OCD (Obsessive Compulsive Disorder). These disorders do not happen or affect you immediately; rather, they gradually develop over time. It is all your fault that you are too protective of your loved one; it is not her fault. Your happiness should be dependent only on you not others. You are entirely thinking incorrectly if you believe that being possessive will make you happy or be good for your relationship. All of it will be destroyed. You might eventually get any mental illness or psychological ailment, but psychological illness is too difficult and painful. The main reality is that a lot of people are unaware that they have any kind of psychiatric disease. You can see how dangerous mental illness is and how it may be deadly. You are unable to tolerate it when the person whom you love now she leaves you; you can't bear it when your beloved departs. Your psychological behavior begins to change as a result of this cause or occurrence since you are overthinking your loved one's departure. Your mental condition will get worse over time as a result of your failure to move past the problem and perseverance in the same thought. This harmful thought stuck a major bad effect on your brain. At this point, your injured brain should start controlling you. The ability to think positively will eventually disappear. Except from this thought other fact is that You seemed and over expected that you and your beloved heart's united in one heart but in reality when she leaves you, you can't control yourself and seems that how you live with one broken heart. The negative thinking capability of brain is activated, you are going to hallucinate. Your negative thoughts again and again hitsyou that you can't live without the person whom you love.

This is the most harmful thoughts or approach in love. If you can feel the real definition of love then you never seem that, those explanation are describe in previous chapter that you never feel depressed and negative thoughts will never affected to you if you feel the purity of love.

There is no condition in love that you will engage as a married couple, but may be destiny isn’t with you. Even if your beloved is unable to get married to you because of family pressure or another major factor, you still need to respect her decision. Love never dies, without engaging with your beloved heartily respect to your beloved this is a part of love.

Love is possible even if you don't tell your lover about it. If you experience those feelings, you will never experience it (depression, anxiety, and finally thinking about suicide). If you love someone, you will be happy for her happiness whether she is with you or not. Your constant prayers for your loved, this is the holiness of love.

However, the issue is that we lack the proper education regarding love and its sacredness, which is why we opted for or appeared to commit suicide. First, we must define what true love is and avoid becoming overly possessive or expecting too much from it.

Remember that being too possessive or expecting too much from a partner can make you mental patient. Always work to overcome these two obstacles so that your happiness will start to depend on you and you won't experience depression.

In love, anything is possible. Therefore, we need to first comprehend about the knowledge of love.

Chapter 5

Remaining single Forever

All we see is that many people—lucky couples—get engaged to their loved ones. those who are involved or connected with the one they love. In the last chapter, we discussed such events and probability.

But a likely incidence is also noted in modern society. It would be incorrect to claim Just in the current society not just in the previous generation, but also in the generation before it. But also, A lots of years ago in love, those events Are also notice. after a breakup or when family pressure prevents you from obtaining your beloved. She May's engaged with other person. And you completely break down yourself. Feels incredibly lonely. And once more discusses depression or love-related sadness, which is also the root of habit.

after a habit. It turns into an addiction. Let's use an example to clarify. A boy and a girl fall deeply in love with one another. They communicate on the phone every day at a specific time or meet each other every day at a specific time. After a few days, those meeting or Speaking becomes a habit. After becoming a habit, addiction results. It becomes so much harmful. Any addiction is similar to hunger. You need have to feed this hunger. However, when two people are in love, the desire to speak or meet completely depends on the other person. It could be for any number of reasons that your beloved is unable to speak or meet with you for even just one day. This means your desire won't be satisfied, which makes you feel extremely melancholy. And some people became really upset over their bad habits and addictions. Addiction and habit refer to a cycle of your desires that you have created. Even a single aspect is not dependent on you. It entirely depends on your loved one.

Additionally, the chemical changes in your brain are visible when the cycle fluctuates or is hampered.

Increased Fluctuation: The person you love unexpectedly ends conversations or meetings. However, if you become dependent on such conduct, you will eventually experience sadness. You become increasingly melancholy as each day passes. Addiction is therefore bad for relationships as well as mental health. This chapter begins by discussing how your beloved May became involved with someone else under familial pressure. It's possible that you and your partner have an addiction, but only those who have the ability to regulate those bitter feelings or emotion. However, the person continues to love his lady love. This person does not injure himself, commit suicide, or experience depression but he may feel little bit of sadness fact is that he can control. However, he is powerless to erase the memories and feelings for his beloved.

"Usne Mujhse pucha

Tum keetab mai kya likhte ho,

Maine bhi haske jawab diya -

Tum likhne ki baat karte ho

Kabhi keetab mai jhaank ke dekhte

Toh apne ankho se aasoon rok nahi paate."

The person then starts to believes that his love might get involved with someone else under familial pressure. But the person still has an inner feeling for his beloved. The person does not publicly express or explain his emotions or feelings for the happiness of his beloved, but he feels that in his hearts she is still with him heartily. The thought of his beloved is starts haunting every time in his mind. The person never gets engaged with anyone. Socially, he spends his entire life remembering his beloved, and everyone around him perceives or observes that he has spent his entire life alone. But for himself, he pays always his life with the feelings, memories of his beloved. He always spends his life internally thinking about his beloved, or externally, he remains alone forever with the memories of someone, means his beloved.

Nobody can predict what will happen in love in the end; everything is possible in Love.

Chapter 6

Achieving Success

Love possesses limitless power. Every chapter includes a discussion of the prospects for love or what happens when it ends. Nobody can foresee the actual possibilities of love. These differ from man to man or from person to person. In love, anything is possible. In the chapter intention of revenge, we covered two options One is positive and other is negative revenging. When a normal person experiences a failure of love or not getting the person whom he loves, they often achieve amazing success. It's a skill for positive revenge. However, there are several cases where a boy falls in love with a girl. They love one another, just like the boy who is average or normal person never has the tendency to achieve amazing success. He is not fully responsible for anything He acts as he would like. He strives to always live in the present and avoid worrying about the future. Another example of modern love. But one is very responsible that he loves his beloved a lot and his beloved also. However, he is not

anxious about the future That how they marry? In this condition, the girl is fully serious about their relationship or to get married. The girl makes an effort to persuade and inspire her adored,
indicates the boy. He can show up on time, but he typically does not show up much or gives the girl or the future top priority. However, the boy is afraid of one thing. Everyone has a weak zone like the boy is not an exception. The boy has a weakness as well. The weak zone is the girl whom he Loves. As a result, he can alter himself out of fear of losing his beloved. When we become attached to someone, it signifies whom

we love. We primarily are unable to fully comprehend this person's. But when will going to lose The Person who is close to our heart. He can feel the value of this person. In this event can alter the boy's viewpoint.

Due to his fear of losing his beloved, he becomes responsible. He can realize that if he does not become a responsible or taking care of a family obligation, at which point he might lose his beloved. This concern, this actuality, or this love from his beloved suggests that if the boy is powerless or incapable of taking responsibility, family pressure may lead her to engage with the other.

Before the situation ever started. The girl persuades and motivates her beloved. His determination, persuasiveness, or dread of losing his beloved, as well as the support of that loved, make him a responsible and successful person.

In love a careless person Can be altered or transformed into a responsible person an unsuccessful human being can be transformed or made successful. Due to the support of love, everything is possible in love. In love, nothing is impossible in love, all possibilities and situations are possible. Nobody can predict what will happen when a relationship ends or after falling in love. In love, anything can happen. Nobody can predict. Love possesses limitless power.

Chapter 7

Too much pious

We talk about love and its ultimate power, which is indescribable in written form. Love is a feeling that no one can express like that the power of love that no one can express. Everything is possible when you're in love. Being excessively devout in love is also a possibility, and it happens in our society all the time. Too good to follow our own religion. When a person falls in love, we suggest that they become extremely religious. Some people who are almost atheists but not completely. The person can be converted to be a piousness person. That is possible in love. Atheist and piousness is in our belief system. However, everyone prays to God when there are no paths to follow.

The Almighty God can do everything. The almighty who creates our destiny, the almighty God can change our destiny. Let's study the reality. In love, couples love They love one another. The boy, for example, is basically an atheist. The girl appears very pious, too. The girl tries to convinces about the believing of God. The boy, though, already denies. However, two different situations could arise in this case: forced or willing. The young boy act to show his faith in God for his beloved. But that's a temporary believing of God, how can an atheist become devout from his own soul? In this situation, if a possibility happen that. They had to leave each other. There is no way for them to come together. The boy has No way or no person can help them to get engaged to them. The youngster has no direction and no one who can assist him. But the girl has that is God by praying.

in the previous. The young lady convinced about God. about the strength of God. Regarding God's generosity, the youngster receives a light from God when he is discouraged, anxious, and unable to find a solution.

He now begins to think that there is someone who can assist him who not only created the entire universe but also has the power to alter fate. There isn't a choice Without praying to God, heartily would then pray to God to marry his beloved. He gradually becomes overly devout as he works towards winning his beloved.

No one can change his mindset about the God, about the believing of God. There is one condition of love, though: the beloved must become extremely religious. Every possibility is possible in love. In love, there is no such thing as an impossibility.

"Tumhe paa naa saka toh kya hua,

Tumhari yaad e toh hai na mere saath.

Aur tumne mujhe kho diya toh kya hua,

Mera dil toh hai na tumahre paas."

Chapter 8

Converts from criminal to humanitarian

Every possible situation is covered in earlier chapters. Let's examine the reality of criminal psychology in relationships.

Many people who commit crimes do so for a variety of reasons, including those related to desires, sadness, anxiety, or revenge (according to the criminal mindset). Etc.

Some people who seek vengeance turn to crime. Each of those is the incorrect strategy. All of those criminal or criminal action is harmful to society and to ourselves. Criminal psychology and psychology in general are very different. Criminal psychology basically follows the criminal path. They lose the capability of thinking, thinking means positive thinking. They are dependent on negative thinking. They don't care whether anyone is harmed. Additionally, it differs from man to man or from individual perspective. Every criminal becomes into a criminal for a reason, however not every criminal is covered by this term. Some of criminal becomes criminal for their desire that's also called psycho. Nobody has the power to change a criminal's attitude. But there is only one way for things to change. It is possible, yes. First, we need to make sure that the criminal is also a human being. They also have feelings and a sense of emotion. This cannot be disputed. How can love transform someone, especially a criminal, into a kind or sociable person? A boy who has committed any non-cognizable crimes?

He has the ability to love too. Suppose, He falls in love with a girl and he shrink into the depth of this girl indicates love. It could take some time to fall deeply in love. A criminal can be a philosopher in love. Being a philosopher without any kind of personal experience is too difficult. After sometime, the boy become extremely possessive in love. Now the boy and the girl falls in love in deep surface, like an animal who does not know how to swimming? The animal is about to sink at this point. How does he save himself? because he is incapable of swimming. The lover mindset experienced a similar situation. if the situation come to the end of his relationship means breakup. As if in the midst of the water, he is currently sinking, or we are quite aware of the possessiveness discussed in the previous chapter. Only a boat can save the animal, like that only getting his beloved can save him or engaged with his beloved means marriage can save him or permanently achieving his beloved can save him. He is dependent on the girl. He will do anything to engage with or get his beloved due to his addiction in love. Now, if the girl wants to make a condition for the benefits of their love or the benefits of their society or the advantages of their future to help him shift from a criminal mindset to a normal or kind person, at this point, everything is possible. He will completely forget that he was a criminal. For the happiness of his loved one and the good of society, he has now cheerfully quit all criminal activity. In his mind and heart, without the girl, no one will stuck. Finally he lives happy life. Yes, there is nothing beyond love. In love, anything is possible. Every possibilities can happen in love without love making generous person from a criminal is impossible. Without love making crime free and generous society is impossible. But we have to define the real meaning of love.

"Where love

There is no place of hatred.

where love

There exists the holiness."

Chapter 9

Luck factor in Love

Everything we learned about love. Possibilities of love, situation after breakup, the harm factor of love, all we discussed, we also discussed about the power of love. How do we comprehend that we fall in love? How do we identify it?

But a factor of destiny that's luck factor also happened in love, only a lucky couple or lucky person can achieve their beloved. Those possibilities are too less. However, only those who are thus lucky can experience these feelings. They are experiencing these emotions of getting their beloved. In genuine love, anything is possible. For individuals who fall in love with a pure heart and have an honest desire to wed. And their goal is to bring their families together in order to be permanently united with their lover. But just a few people can fulfil their desired goals. It implies a marriage, Means engaged permanent by maintaining family, by compromising family. Few couples are able to achieve this.

In those love who are not so possessive or over expected person, they are in limit. They have a deep spiritual love for one another and they possess the true meaning of love. I love you if you are with me, and I don't love you if you aren't. This is a completely incorrect statement or method of approaching love. They have no trust in that place. The person using this strategy. They undoubtedly do not feel or comprehend what true love is.

I love you regardless of whether you are with me or not. Those people believe that this is the proper method of loving. They can find happiness by seeing the happiness in the eyes of their loved ones. They can feel sadness by seeing his beloved eyes tears.

It’s not mandatory to get engaged, but it’s not terms that you will get engaged with that person forever. But your love in your heart will stay in forever, If you feel or understand the real meaning of love, if you love her by your pure heart. Even if your relationship does not result in marriage because of social acceptance, but still have respect for each other. You respect one another. This is the holiness of love. It may be destiny will not allow to unite yourselves, unite your love but still, the respect of each other will still remain forever.

The two spirits may not be able to be united in socially, despite their best efforts. However, in the world of imagination, the souls unite.

No one can feel it 'the union' in the world of imagination. But in another situation, if they engaged means destiny will allow them to unite easily. They do not experience or fear losing their loved one. if they achieve or get their beloved, with trying a lot they will feel those feelings of losing someone or losing their beloved.

Three factors in particular are key in engaging someone.

First one is not so possessive and not so over expected person And Managing family.

A lots of couples sacrifices their love socially, accepting the pain of not getting beloved by seeing their parents or families.

A lots of couple accept the situation of Hell by promising their parents. Many people could be saved from suicide if all families accepted their sons' or daughters' love. Not all love is pure, after all. However, the Guardian may be aware of, judge, and think about their son and daughter's marriage-related decisions.

If Those events happened then, many people do not experience major depression. Many people might live their lives with the person they love. If everyone valued love and understood what it truly meant, no one would ever experience depression.

The final option—the essential one—is God's willing. God has control over everything. You can come together if God wants or you can't if God doesn't wish. But the lucky couple whose wishes get fulfilled. Whose life, subject to God's will, fulfils the three requirements. Socially, they come together, but in whose life the three requirements and God's willingness are not met It becomes impossible to come together. Those in love cannot socially become engaged. But if they feel the real meaning of love still they will never get depressed.

They will respect each other and unites in the world of imagination, only a few lucky couple persons unite or engaged socially. However, people who are unable to achieve acceptance from society they come together in the world of Imagination. And without the couples, nobody feels the union.

“True love and true souls never
come together in reality,

They unite in the world of
imagination.”

Chapter 10

Love

What we think love starts with a sentence of I love you. Absolutely wrong It also depends on individual mindset. In love, I love you This sentence is nothing about formalities. This sentence plays no part in love. Love is a feeling that no one can adequately define. It is entirely described in according to their personal experiences. In love, these feelings That you never gain the same feelings from the other person in the world Without the particular person whom you Love.

How does love create?

Love creates slowly without feels Means you can’t feel that love is going to happen. But when you feel loneliness without the person, you will find yourself by seeing the person. By seeing the person's smile you can smile. Then it is sure that you fall in love. Love is what that you can’t pretend.

when you're alone and miss the person. And you can express all of your emotions—happy, sad, and everything in between—then it is sure that you must fall in love with this person.

Love has no definition, no rules, no limitation. Love is not created by Intention. Love creates by our heart, by our soul. Love is about bringing each other happiness. Love is seeing each other happy. There is no condition in love. One common misconception is that making a proposal is a need for love. You can love without informing her. It is possible.

When you're in love, your eyes can express feelings that only the person can feel.

Love is created slowly not suddenly.

If you get attracted with someone. It calls attraction all we know that. It's not remained in long term. But even notice that attraction also can convert it in love. The person should understand your feelings without telling him. Where love exists, they are ups and down may exist. But revenge and disrespect ness never exist.

Love is love; it cannot be measured by a machine or other tool. Love is love, it may the person is with you or not. Love is in our hand, but to get engaged that is destiny's hand. So we should try to give our best what is in our hand.

Destiny may not Allow to unite. However, if you love someone, you can smile when you see her smile. You will get happiness by seeing your beloved happiness. It may the person is not with you.

In previous describes, Love is in our hand Although union is in the hands of fate, but still, you will be happy, never intend to revenge and respect will remain forever that's called Love.

Last page

In this book, every possibility is presented by a boy, but every possibility is also applicable to girls.

9 798890 262783

Printed by Libri Plureos GmbH in Hamburg,
Germany